THE GLOBAL TRAVELLER SERIES

JAPAN'S TRAVEL CULTURE

SECOND EDITION
expanded by more than 60 pages

The definite guide to the cultural particularities of travelling in Japan

HANS BEUMER

HB Publications
Zug, Switzerland
www.hansbeumer.com

First edition published in July 2017 with ISBN 978-3-906861-22-7, 978-3-906861-23-4
Second edition published in October 2017

This book is available as:
-Softcover: ISBN 978-3-906861-24-1
-EBook: ISBN 978-3-906861-25-8

Printed and distributed by Lulu Press, Inc.

CONTENTS

FOREWORD

Japanese Travel Culture

The Japanese culture differs quite a bit from the Western and other Asian cultures. Within the Japanese culture, the common practices and local travel habits seem to bestow an extra dimension to this culture. This book provides a guide to the particularities of travelling in Japan.

The further away from the big cosmopolitan cities and industrial areas such as Tokyo, Osaka and Yokohama, the more traditional the travel circumstances. Your best travel experiences you will enjoy in the mountainous and rural areas of Japan, where time seems to have stood still.

New in the second edition

This second edition includes the experiences of my eight-weeks travelling through Japan. In August and September 2017, I spent two full months exploring Japan from Hokkaido to Okinawa, travelling 11'000 kilometers (6'800 miles) on planes and trains, by rental cars, buses, metros, trams, taxis, ropeways, ferries and on foot. This new edition provides additional coverage of driving in Japan, local trains, Shinkansen, sightseeing, and many more updates. More than 60 pages and 40 photos have been added.

Benefit of this travel guide

This travel guide for Japan will earn back its cost many times over for you.

It will reduce your time and financial input into a successful trip in Japan by:

- guiding you to realise savings on the travel costs;
- presenting all the relevant travel factors in one definite source.

It will increase your experience and enjoyment output of a successful trip in Japan by:

- optimally preparing for your trip;
- maximising your experience while on location.

The Global Traveller Series

Books published under "The Global Traveller Series" describe the experiences of special and extraordinary travels all over the world. The Series has the intention of helping you advance with your own travel planning, experiences and enjoyment.

Read to advance your life,
drs. Hans Beumer
October 2017

PART I: ACCOMMODATIONS

During your travelling in Japan, you are likely to come across the following accommodations: regular (business) hotel, ryokan, minshuku, shukubo and love hotel. Most of these accommodations can be easily booked through the travel agents or the Internet. The more traditional accommodations in rural areas often require full prepayment. Make sure that you bring those printed accommodation vouchers with you, just in case you need to show them at your check in, although most of the time your passport is sufficient to identify your booking. Some of the accommodations in the more rural areas do not have a presence on English language hotel booking websites, so unless you can read Japanese websites, you will be limited to the travel organisations for these reservations. Many ryokans offer hot spring (onsen) bath experiences. The procedures for taking an onsen bath are particular to Japan and are described in the later sections of this chapter.

Business Hotel

Regular business hotels are available in the cities and larger towns. They are not available in the small villages or locations in the mountains. The regular business hotels provide good value for money and are usually much lower priced than a traditional ryokan. In the business hotel, you will have a normal bed and an ensuite bathroom with your own toilet, sink and bath/shower. It is what you are used to in the West, for example, you do not need to take off your shoes when entering the building. Generally, a meal plan is not included and they do not provide lunch packets, but their restaurant will have extensive opening times for breakfast, lunch and dinner.

The reasonably priced local business hotel chains are often in the direct vicinity of the train stations and may be called Tokyo REI Hotel, Hotel Nikko, Toyoko Inn, JR Hotel, APA Hotel, or Hotel Hokke Club. Most of the international hotel chains have a presence in the larger cities as well, though they are generally more expensive than these local hotel chains.

Ryokan

A ryokan is an accommodation in the traditional Japanese style. You have your own room, and the size of the room is measured in the number of tatami mats covering the floor space. In such a room, you often have a low table, a floor seat with a cushion, a safe for your valuables, a heater or air-conditioning and a TV, and at the front towards the window a little table with two low chairs. All doors to and in the room are sliding doors.

In the more expensive ryokans you have a toilet, shower/bath and sink ensuite to your own room. In other ryokans, you might have only a toilet and sink ensuite to your room. The latter is often the case when you are at an onsen, where the bath and washing facilities are centralised and shared with all guests at the hot spring area inside the ryokan.

There will be one or two wardrobes, with sliding doors as well. The largest wardrobe will store the futons, pillows, futon sheets and blankets, so that these are out of sight during day time. Housekeeping will prepare your futon while you are at dinner. They will put the low table and floor seats in a corner and lay out the futons in the middle of the room.

Meals are served either in your room, or in the ryokan's restaurant. The ryokans provide accommodation, dinner and breakfast as well as a lunch box for the overnight guests, usually in one package price.

Ryokans can be relatively expensive but are an excellent way of experiencing the traditional Japanese culture, food and hospitality.

Minshuku

A minshuku is an accommodation where you do not have your own room in the traditional sense, but where the sleeping space for guests is separated by sliding doors. You leave your shoes behind the front door, before you step on the elevated floor with the tatami mats. In such a 'room' you only have a futon, blanket and a basket with your towel and yukata. There are no locks on the sliding doors and you do not have a safe for your valuables. The shower and toilet are at the back of the building and have to be shared between all the visitors, and with the owners as well. Meals are taken by the visitors together in a separate room. There is little to no privacy as during daytime the sliding doors will be open.

The minshuku provides accommodation, dinner and breakfast as well as a lunch box for the overnight guests, usually in one package price.

A minshuku is a relatively inexpensive way of organising your accommodation while traveling in Japan. The lack of privacy is compensated by the low pricing of a night's stay. It is a good way to get in contact with the local people (hosts and other travellers), though quite often the hosts speak little to no English.

Shukubo

A shukubo is a temple-inn run by monks and provides accommodation, dinner and breakfast for the overnight guests. The stay in a temple-inn is an extraordinary experience that should not be missed during your stay in Japan. All rooms have tatami mats and sliding doors. Often there is no TV in the room. The sliding doors have no locks, but the room has a small safe for valuables. The table is low, and there are no chairs, as you sit on a cushion with crossed legs or with your legs under the low table. The check-in office is like that as well. Several monks do the administration, sitting behind the low tables surrounded by binders and paperwork, but also have a laptop in front of them.

Most tourists travel in groups and share a large room per group. That means that in one room multiple futon mats are placed next to each other, each covered with a thick blanket against the cold. Each room does have a heater, and the low table has an electrically heated blanket underneath, with which to cover your folded legs.

All shoes are left in a rack outside, at the entrance of the building. You get to wear the one-size-fit-all slippers for all indoor walkways. The slippers are left outside the rooms in the hallway; do not wear them in your room.

Dinner and breakfast are served either in the room or in a common room. The meals are Buddhist vegetarian, called Shojin Ryori, and include a soup dish, a grilled dish, a pickled dish, a deep-fried dish, and a tofu dish. They do not provide lunch packages.

The rooms have no toilet, sink or bath; these facilities are separate, and shared between all the guests, but separated for men and women. The bathroom has the low plastic seats and the water tap low at the wall, and may only be used till 9 p.m., after which it closes and cannot be used in the morning. The toilets at the bathroom may include the old squat type toilets, however, there may also be other modern toilets closer to the guest rooms. These modern toilets have the seat heating and bottom-washing water spray.

As in all ryokans, you do not wear your shoes inside but you wear house slippers, in the one-size-fit-all, which means that they frequently slip off your feet when ascending or descending the stairs. In the bathroom, these house slippers are exchanged for toilet room slippers.

The accommodation will also offer a wash room, where you can wash your face, hands and upper body. All guests share these bathroom and toilet facilities.

The overnight price at a shukubo can be at the same level of a ryokan.

Compared to the number of business hotels, ryokans and minshuku, the number of shukubo is very limited. If you want to stay in a temple-inn run by monks, you will need to travel to specific Buddhist temple locations, for example in Kyoto, Nagano or Koyasan.

The whole building will be made of wood, with some walls made of clay. Some shukubo have a beautiful courtyard garden to promote tranquillity for the mind.

Many temple-inns offer day time courses for calligraphy, meditation, and other activities.

The highlight of the stay at the temple-inn is the attendance of the morning prayers and meditation of the monks. The prayer room is divided in two parts; one part for the tourists with a number of small seats, and the other part where the monks have their shrines, statues and perform the prayers. Shortly before 6 p.m., as well as 6 a.m., a monk sounds a gong several times to call all monks for prayer. The morning ceremony can be watched by the tourists. It is very special to hear the chanting, accompanied by the ringing of a bell and a gong for almost an hour and a half. The room is lit by several candles and to the right side a monk keeps a fire burning with small pieces of wood.

In each guest room, as well as in the ante-room to the meditation room, there are long flat wooden sticks (called Ema) on which you can write your name and prayer or wish. You pay a small amount for having such wish-sticks used in prayers and burned in the fire. The dimmed light, candles, incense and chanting of the monks bring a special mystique to the temple room. After 40 minutes, one of the monks will ask the watching guests to follow him, and he guides them in a row through the prayer area, while the monks keep chanting. You get a good close up of the religious objects in the area. The ceremony ends at 7:30 a.m. and breakfast is served from 8 a.m., after which most tour groups and travellers check out.

Love Hotel

A love hotel is an accommodation that is normally rented by the hour by the local Japanese people. Particularly young couples use these love hotels to find intimacy and privacy that is not possible in the small homes of their parents. These love hotels can, however, also be booked for the whole night, at very reasonable prices. A stay at such love hotel is a special experience.

It is adults only access, and the lobby may look like a small discotheque, with dance music, colourful disco lights and a disco ball at the ceiling. In the love hotel in Himeji (Hyogo Prefecture) that I stayed in, the lobby offered several things: a lit-up display of all the rooms with hourly prices; a cupboard with playful costumes for women (e.g., waitress, nurse, school uniform) that can be taken to the room; a selection of soaps and shampoos that can be taken to the room in a small basket (although there was already soap and shampoo in the room that I stayed in); a wide selection of manga books. My room was very spacious, larger than a regular hotel room, as it had a large whirlpool tub in the bathroom. At the head of the bed was a control center for the lights and music. There was a large flat screen TV that offered a few Japanese TV channels, but a wide selection of sex channels. On the bedside table, there were neatly wrapped sterilised women sex toys.

As you can imagine, the love hotel has no restaurant. The small breakfast was served in my room. The room has no windows, as the outside of the windows is covered with flashy advertisement. At night, the outside of the love hotel was lit with a warm red colour.

Onsen

In the mountainous areas, there are many locations which have an onsen, a natural hot spring. Certain mountainous tourist locations specialise in the hot spring baths, and most of the ryokans in these locations have an inside as well as an outside hot bath. These accommodations are very popular with the foreign as well as Japanese tourists, so make sure that you book your stay well in advance. The ryokans with the onsen are more expensive than those without a hot spring, however, it is worthwhile to book a stay there.

Some hotels and ryokans have strict regulations for the use of their public baths. You may read signs at the entrance to the bath, or in the instructions in the room, that people with tattoos are not allowed access to the public bath.

The bigger hotels and ryokans have private baths next to their shared public hot spring baths. In most cases the private bath needs to be reserved at the reception. The key needs to be picked up 5 minutes prior to the start of the reservation, and returned at the end of the reserved time. The reservation time is 45 or 50 minutes from the whole hour. Staff will need 10 to 15 minutes to clean the area and prepare the bathroom for the next guests. The private bath eliminates the separation of the sexes. This means that you and your partner can enjoy the same bath together.

Yukata

The bathing procedures at the onsen are rather special. In your room you find two towels: a regular bath towel, though of small size, and a small towel wrapped in a plastic bag. You also find a Yukata (ankle-long cotton bathrobe), quite often in multiple sizes, in a basket in your wardrobe.

Before leaving your room, take off all clothing (though you can leave on the underwear if you prefer) and put on the Yukata and tie it with the obi band around your waste. In the wardrobe you will probably also find a thick, but short (till the waste), wool Yukata, which you can wear over your long cotton Yukata, in case it is cold or when you want to formalise the dress up. When leaving your room, you slip in the one-size-fits-all house slippers, and with the two towels in your hand, you walk over to the public hot spring bath. In this case public means shared with the other hotel guests.

Noren

The bath area is separated for men and women, and the colour of the noren (a traditional fabric divider, usually having one or more vertical slits and hanging in front of an entrance), will determine which entrance you have to take. A blue coloured noren shows the men's entrance, a red coloured noren shows the women's entrance. At most Onsen the noren will be switched at midnight, so that the bathing area is swapped every day. Not only the entrances are separated between the sexes, but so are the changing areas and the baths. There is no commingling.

Changing room

Behind the sliding entrance door, there is an open shoe cabinet, where you leave your slippers. Barefoot you step on the elevated floor of the changing room, which will have multiple sinks and a rack with open baskets. Sometimes there are no open baskets but instead lockers which can be closed with a key which you take with you in the hot spring bath. You undress and put your Yukata, medium sized towel, and room/safe key in the open basket. The unused baskets are upside-down.

You are naked and take the small towel with you in the bathing area. The first thing you will notice, after opening the sliding door to the hot spring, is the smell. There is the distinct smell of rotten eggs, caused by the sulphur odour which comes with the hot spring water from deep in the earth.

Washing

But you cannot step in the hot bath yet, first you need a thorough wash. For this purpose, the wall is lined with 'washing stations'. Each small station has a hot/cold water tab, a shower head, liquid body soap, shampoo, a small bucket and a small seat. All the Japanese men (and the women as well) sit down on the small seat, and then in a repeating process fill the small bucket with water and empty the bucket over their head and body. Then they soap their hair and body, which they rinse off again by emptying the small bucket. They use the small towel for washing and scrubbing their body. Once all the soap is rinsed off, you can enter the hot bath.

But where to leave this small towel? The Japanese resolve this by folding the small towel and putting it on their head while they are in the bath.

Tub

The hot spring water comes to the surface with a temperature between 60 and 90 degrees celsius (140 to 194 degrees fahrenheit), and is mixed with cold water to achieve a bathwater temperature of around 42 degrees celsius (108 degrees fahrenheit). As a result, all windows and mirrors will be steamed up and the whole inside bathing area is humid. The bath itself is shallow, having a depth of maximum 60 centimeters (2 feet). When you are sitting on your bottom, the water reaches just above your shoulders and your body (till your neck) is submerged, providing super relaxation of your muscles and bones in the hot water.

There is an intermediate step to get into the bath, and when you sit on this step, you can submerge your legs but your upper body stays above the water, which makes it less hot and better to endure.

Some baths are made of wood, some of marble and some of stone, but all show the signs of years of hot spring water and humidity. You will not find the cleanness that you have in your own bath at home, as the many years of humidity and natural minerals contained in the water leave their sediments and traces on the edges of the bath, the overflow areas and the floor, windows and walls.

It is a great way to the end of your day and to relax your body. If there is an outside bath, try that one as well, because the Sulphur smell will be a lot less and the area will be a lot less humid, making the hot water temperature more bearable for your bodily circulation.

After the bath, the Japanese men (and the women as well) perform the same washing routine, before getting back to the changing area.

You will see the Japanese, as well as the foreign tourists, wear the Yukata at the hotel's public areas, such as the restaurant as well.

At some special locations, there may also be public Onsen, freely accessible. Such Onsen can be directly at the riverbed, at a spot where the hot spring water surfaces directly into the river. A screen may protect the views from the street.

Various Experiences

Length

At most of the traditional ryokan accommodations, the door-opening to the room, as well as the sliding doors in the room, have a height of only 1.75 meters (5.74 feet). So, when you are taller than that, duck your head when entering.

Futon

At the ryokan, you sleep on the floor on a futon. The futons are very thin matrasses. Lying on one futon directly on the tatami mats is rather hard. You will like it when you are used to a hard matrass at home. But when you need softness, ask housekeeping to put multiple futons on top of each other. The futon may have a length of only 175 centimetres (5.74 feet). If you are taller than that, your heels and feet will be on the floor.

Pillow

At most ryokans, not only the "bed" is hard, but also the pillows are hard. The pillows are mostly of small size filled with cherry pits. They hardly adapt their shape when your head or neck is resting on it.

Blanket

The thickness of the blankets in the ryokan and other accommodations are always the same, independent of the time of year. It may be 33 degrees celsius (91 degrees fahrenheit) outside, but housekeeping will still cover the futon or bed with a thick winter duvet. You may have to either keep the room cool with the air conditioning, or remove the duvet, to create a comfortable sleeping temperature.

Room lock

Often the door to your room does not automatically lock when you pull the door closed. You need to turn the lock with your key in order to lock it.

Toilet

The toilet at your accommodation will be very comfortable. The toilet seat will be heated and you can clean your bottom with an automated warm water spray. But be aware that some of the public toilets or accommodations in the rural areas may have the old-fashioned squatting toilets.

Wi-Fi

Quite often the traditional accommodations in the more rural areas have Wi-Fi only in the lobby. I was in several ryokans which had no Wi-Fi connection in the room, or where the Wi-Fi access in the room was a Prefecture's free Wi-Fi connection, for which a separate registration from the hotel's Wi-Fi was necessary. So, do not expect seamless access to Wi-Fi in all areas of your accommodation when you are travelling to the more rural areas. Surprisingly, at the temple-inns, the monks had set up very good Wi-Fi connections, covering all areas, including the guest rooms. At a minshuku I could only get access to Wi-Fi when I went close towards the front door.

TV

In most of your accommodations you have a TV in your room. But do not get your hopes up for HBO, Cinemax, or any other English language channel for that matter. The number of channels will be limited to nine, and all will be in Japanese.

Household staff

You will see that most of the household staff are of an elderly age, particularly in the more remote mountainous regions. You will not meet a lot of young people at those locations because of the ageing of the Japanese population, and because young people leave the area to study and work in one of the bigger cities.

Cooling and heating

Because the summers are hot and humid, most accommodations have an air-conditioning system in the guest rooms, which can be used for cooling as well as heating. Some older and more traditional accommodations may not have that, but at minimum will have a gas heater, which does leave a smell and the burning flames make a sound. I can imagine that such gas heaters are a common cause for fires in those wooden buildings. So be careful.

Slippers

Inside the traditional accommodations, you do not wear your shoes; you leave them at the entrance area on a rack. You will need to wear slippers inside the building, and most slippers are one-size-fit-all, without distinction between male, female or foot size. Because they are made of smooth plastic, you will often lose them, particularly when ascending or descending the stairs. In the toilet area, you change slippers: a separate pair of 'toilet slippers' will have to be used. You do not wear the slippers on the tatami mats, meaning that you leave the slippers in front of your room and in front of the restaurant. You also put your slippers on a rack at the entrance of the onsen hot spring bath. Staff will neatly arrange all shoes at the entrance area, and even place a room number next to the shoes.

Luggage forwarding and storage

In case you are travelling with heavy or bulky luggage, which you do not want to or cannot carry during your day hiking or sightseeing, you can make use of the luggage forwarding service. This is a reservation system providing a shuttle service, bringing your luggage from one accommodation to another. The "takuhaibin" is a very convenient way of travelling in Japan, without self-carrying your heavy luggage and big suitcases on trains, buses or metros. The costs of the forwarding services are fairly reasonable, depending on the size and weight of the luggage and the distance. Most delivery is next-day delivery. All major airports have luggage forwarding counters to deposit your luggage. The accommodation can also be helpful in organising the transfer to your next location.

Luggage storage is available at most train stations and most larger bus terminals. Automatic coin lockers offer several sizes, and cost between 300 and 600 Yen (2.70 and 5.30 USD) until midnight. Some locker areas might close at a fixed time (e.g., 8 p.m.) in the evening.

PART II: FOOD

Restaurants

Specialisation

The majority of the restaurants in Japan serve all sorts of Japanese dishes, and many of these specialise in local food. You will mostly find restaurants that offer only one or two types type of food. For example: sushi, sashimi, and tempura; yakitori; shabu-shabu; ramen; soba; sukiyaki; udon; or teppanyaki, and so forth.

Sampuru

When you stroll by the restaurants in the malls and streets you will see their menu choices (and prices) on display in the window. The displays are plastic replicas called sampuru (sample). The restaurants make the menu displays look tasty and many of the dishes look very real. Window shopping at restaurants is fun to do and provides a great help for selecting your meal, particularly when the menu is only in Japanese language.

Second and third floor

Because of the limited ground floor space in commercial buildings and city centres, most restaurants and bars are on the 2nd, 3rd, 4th or higher floor in the shopping and entertainment streets. These restaurants have flashy neon signs and their menus displayed at the entrance to the building or in the street in front of the building. What looks like an office building in a shopping street may actually turn out to be a collection of restaurants and bars at a closer glance. You may have to climb narrow stairs, but almost always the food tastes great, in a cosy restaurant vibrant with activity. You will come across many Japanese office workers engaged in their after-work social team building on the company's expense account.

Smoking

Unlike in many other Western countries, smoking is allowed in the restaurants, so do not be surprised of a blue haze in a small restaurant.

Air-conditioning

The vibrant activities make such restaurants a warm place, which is why all restaurants have their air-conditioning set at about 16 degrees celsius (61 degrees fahrenheit), and cold air blazes above your head. It may be nice for a while when it is hot outside, though be careful with accepting a seat right below a vent. This caused me to get a cold and a slight fever several weeks into my two months' journey.

Technology

Technology has reached many restaurants. You may be able to order by entering your choices from a tablet on your table. I was also in a restaurant where you had to select a menu from a machine, pay at this machine, and with your ticket receive the food. Many restaurants have a bell on the table. Push the button and the waiter will come to you.

International fast food

The number of international restaurant chains is clearly in the minority. You will find the usual American fast food chains spread all over the country, as well as Italian pizza and pasta restaurants.

Ryokans

In most of the traditional ryokan accommodations you can have a meal plan, including breakfast, and dinner and perhaps a lunch box, when you have chosen this package as part of your reservation. Dinner, on the evening that you arrive, and breakfast, the next morning before you depart, are the traditional Japanese set meals. The Japanese breakfast and dinner are served with many small portions of different types of food. At dinner you are likely to be getting a small barbeque or hot pot bowl which is heated and where your meat or small fish is grilled, rice is cooked (sometimes with peas), or soup is boiled.

The meals for the travel group will be served all at once. When you enter the ryokan's restaurant at the pre-set time of your meal, part of the pre-set meal will already be on the table. When you travel alone, you get a small table for yourself. Often your name or room number is displayed on a card on the table, or even at the restaurant door, in case the ryokan has multiple rooms where meals are taken.

Choice

At the ryokans there is usually no menu or à-la-carte choice for food. At some of the ryokans you can, however, choose between a Japanese or a Western set breakfast. Chose the Japanese set meal, enabling you to taste and experience the local ingredients, and have a high protein, low carbohydrates meal.

Your only choices for drinks are beer, sake, soda or tea. Generally, they do not serve coffee, neither after dinner, nor at breakfast, but there is always an unlimited supply of green tea. Most rural accommodations, that are used to hikers, do not serve lunch. Their restaurant will be closed during lunch time. In case you are spending the day at the accommodation, for example, because of heavy rainfall, you will probably need to go outside for lunch, or request the lunch box the evening before.

Times

At the ryokans, the meal times are very strict. Upon your arrival and check-in, you will have to make a choice at what time you want to have dinner and breakfast.

Good Morning, Dear Guests

様　　　　部屋名（　　　　　　）

May I ask you some questions about your schedule today?
（本日のお客様のご予定をおたずねしたいのですが？）

1, What time will you go out today? Thursday
（何時にお出掛けになりますか）
(✓)Around(8.30)am.（大体何時頃） bus
( )Not decided yet.（まだ決めてません）
( ) In the room all day.（外出しません）

2,Do you hope the room cleaning after going out?
（外出された後　お部屋のそうじしましょうか）
(✓) I hope the room cleaning.（して下さい）
( ) Not hope（しないでいい）
( ) Don't enter in the room.（部屋に入らないで）

3,What time do you like to start Dinner tonight?
（今晩の御夕食は何時になさいますか）
(7)p.m. (5:30 ~ 7:00)
And also to start Breakfast tomorrow morning? = Friday
（明日の御朝食は何時になさいますか）
( ) a.m.(7:00 ~ 8:30)
If You Hope continental Breakfast,You can order It.
Japanese style or continental style

The choice for the dinner time is usually 6, 6:30 or 7 p.m., and for breakfast 7, 7:30 or 8 a.m.

Most traditional accommodations show no flexibility for enabling meals outside these times. If you leave before 7 a.m., you will not be able to get an earlier breakfast.

Lunchbox

If you want a lunch box for the next day, you need to request one before dinner time the previous evening. The lunchbox itself contains mostly rice, perhaps with some omelette (tamago) and pickles. Because you will likely carry the lunch box in your backpack, it is good that it only contains dry food. Having a lunch box day after day, however, very quickly becomes monotonous. You have rice for breakfast, lunch, and dinner. At least during breakfast and dinner there are many other small dishes, but in your lunch box it is almost only rice balls.

Department Stores

You do not feel like eating out or want to limit your lunch, dinner or breakfast costs? Visit the B1 or B2 levels of the large department stores and select your meal components to take back to your hotel room or eat outside on a bench. Department stores and supermarkets provide low-priced, good quality Japanese food.

All major department stores, such as Takashimaya, Daimaru, Mitsukoshi, Isetan, and SOGO, have a food department at their B1 (Basement 1) level, and often a large food supermarket at their B2 level. Both levels provide fresh food for take-away. From the ground floor of these department stores, take the escalator down and be amazed by the choices of typical Japanese food, drinks and deserts. At the B1 level there might be some small restaurants where you can sit down, but most of the food stalls are for takeaway. You can find large varieties of sushi, sashimi, salads, and fried food such as tempura, fish, meat, but also sweets, deserts, cake, and drinks such as wine, sake, and fresh juices. You will comingle with many elderly Japanese who are in search of their evening meal, which they put together by buying food from several different food stalls.

The B2-level supermarkets offer fresh food ingredients as well as the usual packaged food, snacks, drinks, and so forth. Go to the fresh fish area, and you will find pre-packaged sushi and sashimi, ready for takeaway. You can find bento boxes with 10 pieces of mixed sushi for as little as 850 Yen (7.60 USD). At the cash counter they will give you chopsticks and one or two packets of dry ice to keep the bento box cool. Small wasabi, ginger and soy sauce packages are normally already included in the bento box. If you are looking for your dinner or next day's breakfast, be sure to arrive at the supermarkets before 6 p.m. When you arrive later in the evening, there is a high possibility that the fresh takeaway meals have already been sold out to the elderly Japanese hunting for food bargains. The closer to closing time, the bigger the chance that this type of fresh food is discounted; if anything is left by that time.

The department stores open from 10 a.m. and generally close at around 8 or 9 p.m. So you will need to get your breakfast the night before, and store it overnight in the refrigerator in your hotel room.

The one or two highest floors (at the level 5, 6, 7, or 8) of the department stores are usually filled with restaurants. Most of the restaurants will be Japanese, with an occasional Italian or Chinese restaurant. Some department stores may have a food court, lined with low-cost fast food counters.

Convenience Stores

Three convenience stores have an extensive network of small supermarkets all over Japan: 7-eleven, Lawson and Family Mart. In total there are more than 50'000 of such stores, providing a convenience store at almost every street corner in the cities. Though most of them are relatively small, they do offer a selection of drinks, snacks, packages food, and fresh refrigerated food. You will find the drinks that you want (including coffee and alcoholic drinks such as beer, wine and sake), but the choice for meals is rather limited. Their price level is very competitive. For example, a regular coffee at 7-eleven costs half the price of a comparable Starbucks coffee. These convenience stores offer no possibilities to sit down.

At the larger supermarkets you will find the same selection of fresh food for takeaway as in the B2 levels of the department stores.

Fish Markets

The freshest and best-priced seafood (sushi, sashimi, oysters, crab, lobster, tuna, and so forth) you will find at the fish markets. Many cities have fresh fish markets where the catch of the day is sold to restaurants and wholesalers from 2 or 3 a.m. in the morning. In Sapporo visit the Nijo market close to the Sapporo TV tower; in Osaka visit the Kuromon market with 500 meters of street aligned with 150 small fresh fish, beef, vegetables and fruit stores; in Tokyo visit the Tsukiji's outer market.

But you do not need to get up that early to enjoy the fresh fish. All the fish markets have small and basic restaurants (many with only plastic folding chairs and small tables with plastic cover) that show the fresh fish and seafood and you only need to point to what you want and they will prepare it for you. Blowtorched crab legs, fresh oysters opened in front of you, freshly prepared sushi and sashimi, live eel, sea urchin, and so forth. It is great for breakfast, lunch or dinner if you do not mind the basic setting of most stores.

Train Stations

The train stations provide another good source for meals. Many of the train stations in Japan encompass department stores, restaurants and shops, bakeries, coffee shops, and small convenience stores, offering a wide variety of choices for shopping, dining and entertainment. For example, Kyoto station is one of Japan's largest buildings, a giant modern construction of glass and steel, including a department store, hotels, and many restaurants and shops.

Though traditionally the Japanese do not eat bread, many bread stores have popped up in the large train stations. You can find freshly baked breads in many types and flavours. Interestingly, all of these bread stores have French names. You do not order the bread at a counter, but you take a tray and large tweezers, and select your choices of bread from openly stored displays (not very hygienic) in the store. Then you pay at a normal cash counter, where they wrap the bread in many plastic bags (not very environmental). Often they only accept cash.

Vending Machines

The traditional guest rooms in the accommodations usually have a refrigerator, but it is almost always empty. You can buy your cold drinks from the vending machine in the lobby of the accommodation. You can buy beer, sake, as well as sodas, cold coffee and mineral water; whatever you need in your room or to take away for your day sightseeing or hiking.

In the streets, at the train stations, at the tourist sightseeing spots, at the bus terminals, at any place where people frequently pass, you will find the cold drinks vending machines. Hot drinks or hot meals vending machines are very rare.

You may also come across some non-food vending machines, such as the underwear vending machine that I saw on the 5th floor of my hotel in Shingu (Wakayama prefecture).

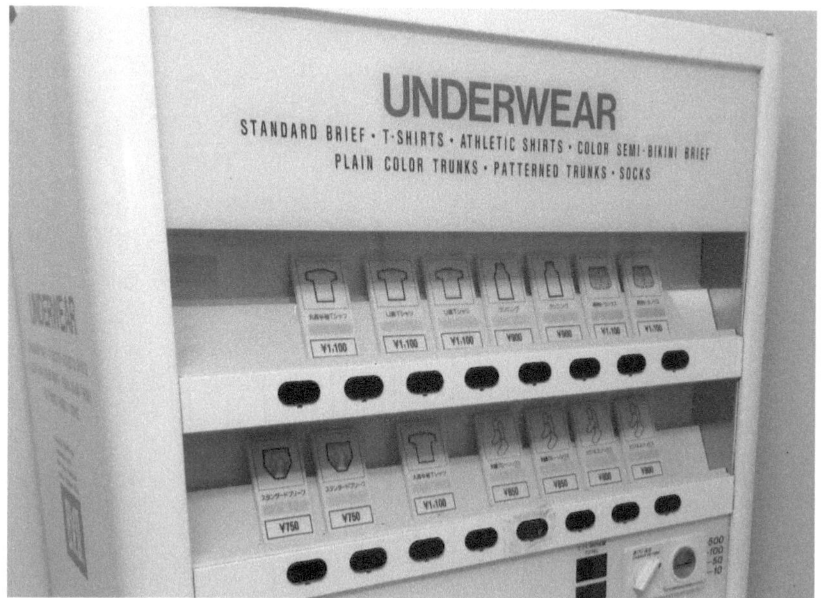

PART III: TRANSPORTATION

Domestic Flights

JAL and ANA dominate the domestic flight market with moderate to expensive priced air tickets. In case you are travelling on a low budget, two ways are available for containing your inland flight costs.

Low cost airlines

Like in any other country, Japan also has a number of low-cost airlines, for example: Skymark Airlines, Vanilla Air, Jetstar Japan, or Peach Aviation. These low-cost airlines provide excellent value for money when compared to JAL and ANA. For example, a ticket with Vanilla Air from Naha/Okinawa to Tokyo/Narita cost me only 8'360 Yen (75 USD), even though it was booked only one day in advance, and the flight had a duration of

2 hours and 30 minutes (compared to an ANA ticket of 475 USD for a one day in advance booking). This low cost compensates for departing from or arriving at a remote airport terminal (for Vanilla Air at Naha: the airport's cargo area, with the check-in and waiting in a poorly restyled cargo warehouse).

Special tourist fares

Make use of ANA's low-cost foreign tourist fares, with the fare base called ANA Experience JAPAN, Super Value. This special fare is available when:

- booking at least three days in advance
- reserving and purchasing through the ANA website
- holding a non-Japanese passport and your residence is outside Japan (passport information must be entered upon booking)
- holding an international flight ticket to and from Japan (ticket code or reservation number must be entered upon booking)

With the ANA's Super Value (ANA Experience JAPAN Fare), all the domestic flights have a standard fare of 10'000 Yen (87 USD), plus around 1'000 Yen (9 USD) for taxes. For example, I purchased a ticket from Tokyo/Haneda to Sapporo/Hokkaido for only 11'000 Yen (USD 98), and a ticket from Naha/Okinawa to Tokyo/Narita cost me only 11'000 Yen as well (travelling in August and September 2017).

Trains

Riding the train in Japan is easy, and very similar to other countries. There are, however, several particularities you should be aware of.

Rotating benches

All Shinkansen trains, as well as most regional express trains, have two- or three-seat benches that can be turned around. Whenever the trains arrive at their terminal station, the train staff or the passengers turn the benches into the new direction of the train. A pedal at the isle-side of the benches needs to be pushed down to unlock the rotating undercarriage. The benches can then be easily rotated to face the new direction of travel. This way, all benches always face forward and the travellers always face the direction of travel.

When travelling in a group of more than two or three people, it is possible to turn the benches so that you can face the other travellers (who then ride backwards). Families with children often do this.

Display and announcements

All Shinkansen trains, as well as most regional express trains, display information about the upcoming stops in Japanese as well as in the English language above the doors of the passenger carriages. From your seat, you are able to see when your station is coming next. Prepare to exit quickly because those trains only make a brief stop. The same information is also called in announcements in Japanese and English language prior to each stop.

Smoking

Although most trains are smoking-free, most Shinkansen have one carriage where smoking is still allowed. When you make your seat reservations, make sure that you do or do not (depending on your preference) reserve in the smoking compartment. A few regional Shinkansen have smoking rooms instead of smoking cars.

Japan Rail Pass

The JR pass can only be purchased outside of Japan and in advance of your travels. You can order it from travel agents in your local country. You do not actually buy the JR rail pass itself, but rather an exchange order for such a pass.

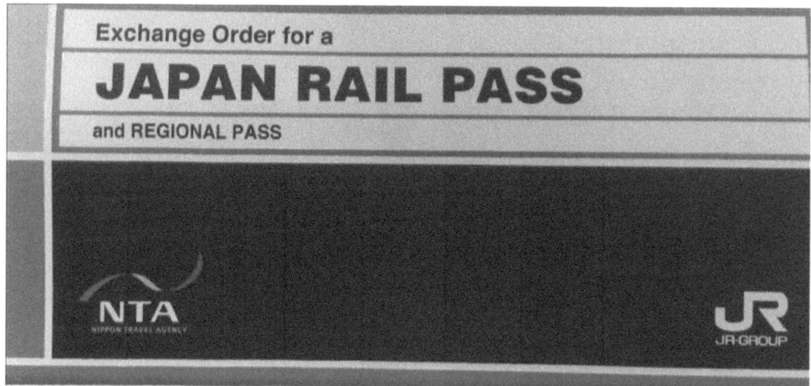

When you arrive in Japan, you have to go to a JR ticket office (at the airport or at any train station) in order to exchange the ticket. It must be exchanged within three months of issuance, so do not purchase it too long in advance of your trip to Japan. You will need to show the "temporary visitor" stamp in your passport. At the exchange you need to determine the starting date of the pass. You then can only use the pass from its starting date for the duration of the pass (7, 14 or 21 days). The first time you use your pass, the station clerk at the ticket gate to the tracks will put a stamp (seal) with the date of entry.

These passes can be for 7 days, 14 days or 21 days. Are you staying longer in Japan? Then buy two passes. For example, during my eight-weeks trip in Japan, I purchased a 7-days and a 21-days rail pass. The rail passes have fixed prices of 29'110 Yen (250 USD), 46'390 Yen (405 USD) or 59'350 Yen (520 USD) respectively (for one adult, ordinary seat, prices in 2017). These passes are excellent value for money. The passes let you ride unlimited on the JR trains all over Japan, without having to pay for any single ticket or seat reservation.

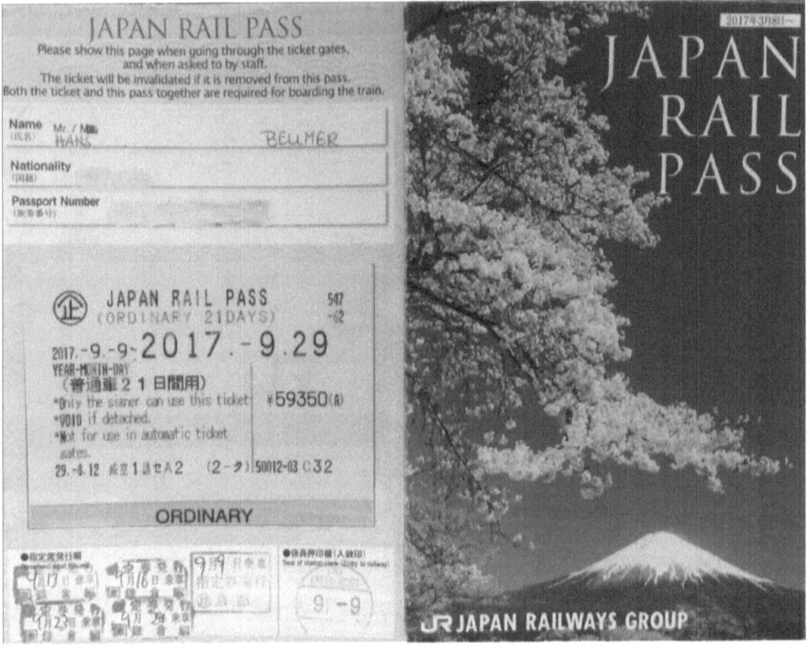

Two limitations exist:

1. The JR pass cannot be used for the private trains, only on the Japan Rail routes. You need to buy separate tickets for these private railways, for example from Odawara to Gora in the Hakone national park, south of Tokyo. It cannot be used on buses or metros either.

2. The Nozomi and Mizuho Shinkansen lines cannot be used. If you want to use these, you have to purchase separate tickets.

However, the JR passes can be used on a few JR bus lines and JR ferries, for example on the ferry to Miyajima Island, about 25 minutes by train from Hiroshima.

When you are planning to limit your travel to one or several particular regions of Japan (e.g., Hokkaido, Kansai or Shikoku) you will be cheaper off when you buy a Regional JR pass. These passes are available for up to 5 or 7 days, and may cost between 55 and 230 USD.

HyperDia

www.hyperdia.com is the only English language website for researching and planning your train schedules. It is accurate and up to date for all train schedules, whether Shinkansen, regional express trains or local private trains. Use this website to plan your train travel before flying to Japan. A search on this website, for example from Tokyo to Nagano, will generate several travel options at different times. It will show the duration, the train name and number, the track of departure and arrival (for the Shinkansen trains), the fare, the distance and the number of transfers.

Print out the relevant schedules and bring them to the ticket offices. You only need to show your schedule, and the clerks at the counters know exactly which tickets to give to you. Hyperdia is a research and planning website, not a reservation website. On this website you cannot reserve or buy tickets; they will have to be made at the ticket offices at one of the many train stations in Japan.

Watch the colour coding of the non-Shinkansen train icons on Hyperdia. The JR lines (for which the JR pass is valid) have a green coloured little train icon. A red coloured little train icon represents the non-JR lines, such as the private train companies. As the JR pass is not valid for the private train companies, you will have to buy separate tickets for those red coloured train journeys.

When planning your train trips, you will see that some stations have the prefix "Shin". For example, Shin-Yokohama or Shin-Osaka. "Shin" denotes that it is a train station where the Shinkansen halts. Quite often, these Shin-stations are not the city center stations. For example, it takes a 4-minute JR train ride to get from Shin-Osaka station to Osaka station.

Fares

The train ticket price consists of two components: the fare and the seat fee. The fare is the same for everyone buying tickets. The seat fee depends on your choice of one out of three: green seat (first class), reserved seat or unreserved seat. For example, from Tokyo to Kyoto, the prices are as follows: fare on any of the Shinkansen: 8'210 Yen (73 USD); green seat 10'170 Yen (91 USD); reserved seat 5'390 Yen (48 USD); non-reserved seat 4'870 Yen (43 USD). Thus, the total price of a reserved seat on the Shinkansen from Tokyo to Kyoto is 13'600 Yen (121 USD).

When you carry a valid JR Pass, you can take this train with a reserved seat, without having to pay separately for the fare or seat fee.

As you can see, it takes only two such train journeys within one week (a return trip Tokyo-Kyoto) to match the cost of the 7-days pass. Travel more within one week, and the pre-purchased 7-days JR pass will be cheaper than buying the tickets separately.

Tickets

When you purchase a train ticket without a JR pass, you will get two green tickets (with a black back): the fare ticket and the seat ticket. When passing the ticket gates, you will have to show both the tickets.

When you hold a valid JR pass, you do not need the fare ticket (the JR pass replaces the fare ticket). But when you want to have a reserved seat, you will still need to get the seat ticket at the ticket office, even though you do not need to pay for it separately. When passing the ticket gates, you need to show only the JR pass.

Seat reservations

You have the choice between reserved and non-reserved seats on all Shinkansen and regional express trains. Local trains only have non-reserved seats. The advantage of the reserved seat is that you are guaranteed an assigned seat. On the main Shinkansen, the seats A-B-C are the three-seats benches; the seats D-E are the two-seats benches. Seats A and E are at the small window; C and D are isle;

B is a middle seat. Some of the regional Shinkansen and regional express trains have a configuration of A-B and C-D seats.

The non-reserved cars are usually cars 1 to 5 of the 16-car Shinkansen.

When traveling during peak commuting hours or festive periods, it is worthwhile to reserve a seat, as the non-reserved seats will get fully occupied very quickly and you might end up standing in the isle or corridor for a multiple hour journey. This requires a seat reservation several days in advance. In my personal experience, it is no problem to find empty seats in the non-reserved cars when travelling outside the commuting hours.

The seat reservations are for one particular train at one particular time, fixing your date, train, seat and time of travel.

Frequency

The Shinkansen trains arrive and depart with a high frequency. Some of these trains depart every 10 minutes on the same route. There are so many trains, that you need to wait only a short time in case you missed your train. When you missed your train with a reserved seat, you can still board the next train, but you will have to occupy a non-reserved seat (or go back to the ticket office and change your seat reservation to the next train). It is quite different for the regional and local regular trains. In some of the more rural areas, for example on Shikoku or from Wakayama to the South, most trains run on an hourly schedule. Miss your train, and you will have to wait for an hour.

Glass divider to the driver's cabin

Some of the local trains have a glass divider between the passenger car and the driver's cabin at the frontend of the first passenger car. You can then see the tracks in front of the train, looking through the glass divider through the front windshield of the train. You will see the same as the driver, which is rather unusual. Additionally, you can observe the driver's activities and motions, particularly the Shisa Kanko.

Shisa Kanko

Shisa Kanko is the Japanese name for the procedure of "pointing and calling" to prevent accidents. You may see the conductor or the driver of the train point to the timetable or the signal in an exaggerated way with a stretched arm and hand, and call out "OK" for a confirmation that the train is on schedule or that the driver is appropriately responding to the signals on the tracks. This method of error prevention can only be found in Japan and is interesting to observe. The train drivers and conductors take their pride in this procedure, and though it may seem strange, its underlying error prevention theory is solid, as Japan's railways have one of the lowest numbers of accidents in the world.

Punctuality

The Shinkansen are always punctual and on time. Since they have their own tracks without any crossings, their punctuality has hardly any disturbing factors. So expect your train to leave on time! The same is valid for the regional and local trains. They run with the time precision of Swiss clockworks or Japanese digital watches.

Separate entrance gates

Because the Shinkansen tracks are separated from the regional and local train tracks, the entrances to the Shinkansen platforms are separated as well. The tracks are usually elevated and above the regular train tracks. The entrance and ticket gates may be at the same level as the regular train tracks, but to reach the Shinkansen platforms, you will always have to go up the stairs or escalators.

Bowing

You will see that each time the conductor enters or leaves a carriage he will briefly bow towards the travellers. Train staff on the platform will bow towards the train when a train arrives and departs.

Food and drinks

Only the Shinkansen have a snacks and drinks service, a lady with a trolley going through the train several times each hour. All other trains, even the regional express trains with duration of 3 hours, do not provide such services. So if you travel early morning, around lunch time or dinner time, make sure that you bring your own drinks and food onto these regional trains. All the larger train stations have a selection of food and drink take-outs at the station (before entering the platforms) or on the platforms themselves.

Bins

Although the principle is to take your trash home (see the chapter Trash), the Shinkansen and the regional express trains provide bins next to the exit/entrance doors. If you do not use those for your empty coffee cups, bento box or banana peel, you are likely going to carry this trash back to your hotel room, in case the platform itself does not offer bins.

Speed

The Shinkansen are well known for their speed. Their normal cruising speed is around 285 kph (177 mph) on tracks that are normally elevated, with few curves, and completely separated from the all other passenger and cargo train tracks. Their speed is enabled by: the absence of track crossings; the absence of other slower trains on the same tracks; and the construction of many tunnels that cut through mountains in straight lines. During my 65-minute trip with the Sakura Shinkansen from Hiroshima to Hakata, the train cruised about 80 percent of the time through tunnels.

This speed makes the Shinkansen many times faster than driving a rental car on the Japanese highways.

Rental Cars

Driving in Japan is an experience in itself. Many rental car companies offer good value for money for a rental car. It is a great and flexible way of getting around some areas where the train or bus transportation is insufficiently available or inefficient in terms of locations and frequency. For example, travelling in the Japanese Alps, on Shikoku Island, or in the national parks of Hokkaido is so much easier and relaxing with a rental car. You really do not need a rental car when you are staying within the conglomerates of the big cities and when only visiting the main and popular sightseeing attractions.

Many rental car companies have their office and car park very close to the main train stations. Hence, it is easy to arrive by train, and within a 3-minute walk reach the car rental office.

Getting into the countryside or mountains and national parks with a car will enable you to see and experience Japan in a different way. When planning your self-driving in Japan, you should consider the following.

Left side driving

They drive on the left side. Though I am only used to driving on the right side, it was very easy to adjust to left-side driving. Rent a car with an automatic shift instead of manual to eliminate the problem of shifting with your "wrong" arm (many rental car companies actually only offer automatic gears when choosing a Japanese car brand).

Low speed limits

The traffic in Japan is generally very slow, making it easy to adjust to the left traffic. Speed limits are at 40, 50 or 60 kph in the cities and 70 or 80 kph on the highways (respectively 25, 31, 37, 44 or 50 mph). Only once during my more than 2'300 km (1'400 miles) of self-driving did I drive on a stretch of highway where 100 kph (62 mph) was allowed. However, you will see many locals drive at least 10 to 20 kph (6 to 12 mph) faster than the limit. In the more remote areas, the highways are often only two lanes. When you drive at exactly the speed limit on a two-lane highway, you will be the front car of a slow-moving traffic jam.

Tunnels

If you are claustrophobic and cannot stand the narrow confines of long tunnels, do not self-drive on the rural highways in Japan. There are many tunnels cutting through mountains; sometimes it felt like driving at night instead of in daytime. In the Japanese Alps I had several stretches with many consecutive tunnels of 1, 2, 4, 5 and even 11 kilometers of length (0.6 to 7 miles length).

English language navigation

Make sure that you rent a car with a navigation system that can display and speak in English. Unless you can read and understand Japanese, it is extremely difficult to find your way without English language guidance. Interestingly, you can enter a location's (e.g., a hotel) phone number in the car navigation system: there is no need to type in Kanji characters or their English translation.

Toll roads

Many highway roads (expressways with green signs) are toll roads. For convenience, rent an ETC card, and you can drive through the blue tollgates without having to stop. Upon returning the rental car, the rental car company will read the accumulated toll fees on the ETC card and you can settle the incurred amount by credit card.

Driving permit

You can drive in Japan with an International Driving Permit (IDP) issued in your home country. Several countries, such as Germany, France and Switzerland, do not issue these IDPs based on the 1949 Geneva Convention. If you are from one of such countries, you will need to obtain a Japanese translation of your local drivers license. Such translation can be obtained from the

Japanese embassies/consulates in your home country or more easily at the local JAF (Japan Automobile Federation) office in Tokyo or one of the other main cities (3'000 Yen (27 USD), ready in 2 hours).

Mobile home

A flexible and cheaper alternative to a rental car in combination with hotels can be a mobile home or RV. Several rental companies in Japan offer a good selection of mobile homes, varying in sizes from very small to large. Check out the mini RV on the picture, containing a small (Japanese size) double bed, and a tiny kitchen.

Parking

Parking can be rather expensive and a special experience. It can be expensive because of the limited space in the cities, where it may cost up to 400 Yen (3.55 USD) per hour. At tourist attractions and national parks the parking fees are often a flat amount, up to 600 Yen (5.30 USD). Similarly, hotels often charge a flat fee of around 1'100 Yen (10 USD) for overnight parking. The most unique type of parking is the elevator parking in towers in the city centres. You drive your car on a turntable in front of the parking tower. The operator turns the table so that the car faces the front of the elevator. You drive the car in the narrow car-elevator and get out of the car. The operator will then rotate the elevation mechanism that moves your car up in the tower. When collecting your car, the operator will automatically rotate the lift till your car is at the storage exit/entrance gate of the tower.

Public Buses

Riding the bus is different from what you are used to. You cannot buy tickets in advance, and you do not enter at the front of the bus. Instead you enter through the doors in the middle or at the back of the bus.

Ticket

Upon entering you must draw a small ticket from the ticket machine at the right or left side of the entrance. This ticket is a small stub with a number, representing the bus stop number/location where you entered the bus.

Fare

At the front of the bus, above the windshield, a large electronic table displays the number of each of the bus stops, and below that number the amount of the fare that needs to be paid. For example, if you get on the bus at stop number 11, your ticket number will be 11, and when the bus arrives at bus stop number 12, the amount could be 100 Yen. Upon arriving at bus stop number 13 the amount will increase, for example to 250 Yen, and so forth.

Calling the stops

In some buses this electronic display also shows the names of the upcoming bus stop in Japanese and sometimes in English. At the same time the upcoming bus stop names are called over the loudspeaker by the chauffeur or by a pre-recorded tape, in Japanese and in the tourist areas also in English.

Payment

When your stop is coming up, push the stop button and when the bus halts, walk to the front of the bus. You can read the exact amount to be paid from the display at the front of the bus. Payment is in cash only, so make sure that you carry enough coins and 1'000 Yen notes. Next to the chauffeur there is a changing machine for coins and 1'000 Yen notes. Just insert the note into the machine, and it will spit out the same amount in coins. You insert your number stub together with the correct amount of coins for your bus fare into the register, which records the amount that you paid. You get no receipt or ticket stub.

Fixed fare buses

In the tourist hot spots, for example Kyoto or Hiroshima, some of the short-route city buses or trams have fixed fares. Particularly the city buses or trams that have their routes along the main tourist attractions (for example, the main temples and shrines in Kyoto, or the A-bomb Dome and the Peace Memorial Museum in Hiroshima) charge a fixed fare independent of the distance of your ride and the stop that you exit.

These fixed fares vary between 160 and 260 Yen (1.40 and 2.30 USD).

Day pass

If you are planning to frequently use the city tram or bus network at the tourist location, it is worthwhile to purchase a city transportation day pass, or multiple-day pass. These passes can be purchased at the tourist information office or the bus terminal. Since the staff at the tourist information office speak English and can advise you of the distances, bus numbers, bus stops and travel routes to the main attractions in the city, it is easiest to buy the day passes there.

A day pass may cost between 500 and 1'000 Yen (4.40 and 8.80 USD), depending on the extensiveness of the city's transportation network. As soon as you use the local transportation network three or more times a day, the day pass will be more economical than paying the single ride fares.

No English

The bus drivers speak little-to-no English, but are extremely friendly and will always assist you in case you have difficulties with this system. When the bus is not so full, the driver may even ask you where you want to go and make a special announcement to you when your stop is coming up. You can always walk up to the bus driver and make the special request that he lets you know when your stop is due.

PART IV: SIGHTSEEING

Tourist Information Office

One of the great advantages about travelling in Japan is the extensive network of tourist information offices. Each city or village that has tourist attractions will have a tourist information office to support the Japanese as well as the foreign tourist. Sometimes these tourist information offices are separated for the Japanese and the foreigners, but most of the time they are combined. When they are separated, a sign on the door will indicate in English that the office is for Japanese language only, and that the foreigner's tourist information office is at a close distance.

These tourist information offices are located at the airports and the train stations, bus terminals or even in the vicinity of the main attractions. When travelling through Japan, you will most likely use the tourist information offices at the railway stations. Even the smallest railway station will have such an office, as long as there is a tourist attraction nearby. When exiting the train platform, just look for the signs pointing to the tourist information office.

The staff of the tourist information offices are always extremely helpful. In my experience, it suffices to ask them what the main attractions are and how to get there. They will take out an English language map of the city that includes the locations of the main attractions as well as the easiest public transportation to get there. They will provide you with information about the bus numbers, the bus fares, the duration of the bus ride, which stop to take, the number of minutes to walk from the bus stop to the sightseeing, the entrance fee to the sightseeing, and so forth.

Before you start doing any sightseeing, first visit the local tourist information office at the train station. They will give you a wealth of information, maps, tips and advice on cost, times and transportation, and so forth. Sit down with all this information at the coffee shop at the train station, or take it to your hotel room, and plan your sightseeing for the (next) day(s). This will optimise the use of your time for that location and enable you to see the major sights in an efficient way.

Photography

Many Japanese carry big cameras with long lenses and tripods. They are used to making many pictures, so you will not attract any attention when you make many photo shots with your smartphone or camera. Still, there are some places where it is prohibited to take pictures. These places are the museums and the temples and shrines. Generally it is not allowed to photograph the holy interiors and Buddhist statues at the temples. Similarly, it is prohibited to photograph the sliding door screens in most historical buildings, for example at Nijo Castle in Kyoto.

Free Tour Guides

At some of the main tourist destinations you will find free tour guides for foreigners. Some cities offer the guide services of senior citizens that have a reasonable to good command of English. I made use of such services in Matsumoto (Nagano Prefecture) to view the black castle, and in Ikaruga (Nara Prefecture) to view the Horyu-ji temple complex. These tour guides are proud to explain the national treasures and reveal insight which you will not find in the brochures. It is a nice way to connect with the local citizens.

QR Codes and Audio

Quick Response (QR) code is the square matrix barcode that can be read by the camera of your smart phone, when you have installed the right app. In case you have Wi-Fi, you can read the QR codes at many sightseeing objects (for example, within Osaka Castle, or at museums).

Many museums and sightseeing locations provide foreign language audio devices, explaining the cultural objects on display.

UNESCO World Heritage

UNESCO lists 21 World Heritage Sites for Japan. When you do your travel planning, check out the list and locations, and make sure that you include the sites in your area for a visit.

For example: Himeji Castle, the Temples and Shrines of Nikko, the A-Bomb Dome in Hiroshima, the Itsukushima Shrine, and the Kumano Kodo sites and forest trails.

National Treasures

In Japan, many hundreds of items have been designated as a National Treasure. These items range from castles, Buddhist temples, and Shinto shrines to sculptures, swords, textiles, paintings and historical artefacts. The Kansai region, including Kyoto, Nara, and Koyasan, has the highest number of national treasures because it contained the former capitals of Japan.

Quite a few significant buildings and sites are under long-term (multiple years) refurbishment and maintenance. Therefore, do not be surprised when the main attraction of your sightseeing day is fully wrapped and only limited or no access is possible. Unfortunately, the relevant internet site and brochures do not warn you for such limitations, but some tourist information offices might provide such information.

During your travel planning, check out the listing of National Treasures in the region you want to visit and include them in your itinerary.

National Parks

Japan has more than 30 National Parks and more than 50 Quasi-National Parks. These National Parks boast beautiful landscapes, forests, rivers, lakes, mountains, and so forth. As you will see when travelling through Japan, substantial parts of the country are mountainous and covered with forests. Forests cover almost 70 percent of the country. For example, the Akan National Park in Hokkaido or the Hakone National Park south of Tokyo provide water, mountain and forest activities for locals as well as foreign tourists. They offer great hiking trails and panoramic views on the mountains and lakes.

The volcano's, waterfalls, and trees addressed in the next chapters can often be found in these National Parks.

Nature Worshipping

In the historical religion of Japan (Shintoism), the people worship many aspects of nature: landscapes, lakes, mountains, rocks, the forces of nature, trees, volcanos, waterfalls, and so forth. This worshipping is done at the shrines. You will see this reflected by the torii, shrine entrances as well as the Shimenawa Sacred Ropes. These ropes are placed at sacred entrances to ward off evil spirits or hung around objects to indicate the presence of a sacred spirit.

These ropes have a consistent appearance, consisting of three parts: a long string of rope (nawa) or wound rice-straw around an object that is considered to be sacred; strings of tied straw hanging down from the rope; white paper folded in zigzag shapes (shime) hanging down from the rope.

The tied straw hanging down represents rain (and thus prosperity) for watering the rice fields in ancient times; this may also be seen as a brush to purify or bless worshippers. The white zigzag folded paper is said to represent lightning and symbolises purity.

Volcanos

Japan has more than 100 active volcanos, and the many calderas of these active and dormant volcanos shape the landscapes. The volcanic activities make for spectacular and unique sightseeing of hot spring pools, geysers, gas emissions, and calderas. Explore the uniqueness of volcanic activities during your travels in Japan.

Waterfalls

More than 70 percent of Japan is mountainous, and in combination with a wet climate in many areas, the country offers many spectacular waterfalls. The Japanese Ministry of Environment has even compiled a list of the top 100 waterfalls. During your travel planning, check out the waterfalls in the region you want to visit.

The number 1 waterfall is the Nachi Falls at Nachi Taisha (Wakayama Prefecture), being Japan's highest waterfall, a UNESCO world heritage site, and considered a scared waterfall:

Number 2 is the Kegon Waterfall at Nikko (Tochigi Prefecture), being the most famous waterfall:

The Kegon Waterfall is close to the Nikko World Heritage Temples and Shrines. The morning sunlight can project a beautiful rainbow in the spray of the waterfall.

The country, however, offers many more spectacular waterfalls, for example, at Karuizawa (Nagano Prefecture).

Trees

When you are sightseeing, look at the spectacular large, old and small trees particular to Japan. You will see 1'000-year-old trees that are worshipped like deities at the temples.

You will see impressive 500 to 800-hundred-year-old cedar trees lined along a narrow forest trail leading to a shrine.

You will see pine trees shaped to perfection through the bonsai techniques in temple gardens, public parks, museum grounds and private gardens.

Zen gardens

Many of the Japanese temples and historical complexes offer beautiful zen gardens. You will see beautifully shaped trees, geometrically formed rock gardens, piled up small white stones and ponds with colourful koi fish.

Temples

During your sightseeing, you will come across many temples, oji, jizo, shrines, kannon and other Buddhist religious buildings and statues.

A temple is a building that houses Buddhist statues, and usually has a name that ends with '–ji'. In front of a temple you will usually find incense burners for purification. Many temples are accompanied by a pagoda, a multi-tiered tower. The temple is centred around Buddha and can usually be entered by the visitors and pilgrims. Many pilgrims burn incense sticks in front of the temple.

Shrines

The main purpose of a shrine is to safeguard the sacred objects contained inside the building, while at the same time providing the housing for the deities. A deity is a being that is thought of as holy and sacred. Many shrines have features that are unique to Japan, for example the torii archways, of which there can be one or multiple, often painted in the typical orange colour. The name of the shrine is followed by the word '-jingu'. The visitors and pilgrims cannot enter the shrines. The buildings can only be observed from the outside. In front of the shrines there are troughs filled with fresh water, which are used for purification, cleaning of your hands and mouth before entering. The water comes out of the mouth of a dragon, as the dragon is considered the god of water. Do not swallow the water or touch the large spoons with your mouth though. In ancient times the pilgrims used to purify themselves in the rivers that they had to cross.

The religious procedure at the Shrine is that, after purification, the pilgrim first rings the bell to wake up the deities. Then they toss a small coin (in ancient times rice or vegetables) in the big wooden chest, which is to pay for the wish that is made later. Two bows follow as a courteous greeting, as well as two handclaps, to draw the personal attention of the deities. A wish is made in the mind, not spoken out, finished by one bow to thank the deities for accepting the wish.

Ojis

An oji is a small shrine placed along the pilgrimage routes with the purpose of protecting the pilgrim and providing him guidance as to the right path and trail in the direction of a Grand Shrine. These shrines often house small stone statutes, representing the princes, or children of the deities worshipped at a Grand Shrine. They are the guardians of the pilgrims and provide a place for much needed rest along the hazardous way. For today's hiker, the oji rather represents a marker on the stage of the route, though many Japanese pilgrims still see them as a place of worship as well. These pilgrims pay the oji small coins to thank the guardian for their safety and showing the right path.

Kannon

A kannon is a Buddhist figure, being represented in many temples as one of the most important deities. These little stone statues may, for example, represent the kannon Bodhisattva, the great saviour to those suffering and protector of children in the afterlife. Some of these kannon statues may wear a bib. The bibs are put on the statues by parents who lost children, with the prayer that the Bodhisattva will watch over them. It is a common custom that is often practiced on other Buddhist statues as well.

PART V: OTHER EXPERIENCES

Umbrella

In the big Japanese cities you will see more people carrying an umbrella than in London. The typical transparent rain umbrella is sold at most convenience stores and shops, and is carried by many Japanese commuters independent of the weather forecast. On a most beautiful sunny day, people will still carry them.

Though you need to make the distinction between two types of umbrellas: against the rain and against the sun. On a sunny day, many women will put up their sun-umbrella to prevent their skin and face from tanning. They will wear long sleeves, sun hats and large sun visors to protect them from tanning.

Japan's climate is humid many months of the year, and the rainfall is frequent. As 70 percent of Japan is mountainous, the weather can be unpredictable. During my two travel months (August and September), I regularly experienced low clouds and rain. This may render your sightseeing day a waste of time and money when you expect panoramic views. For example, on the day that I visited mount Fuji, heavy rain and low clouds obstructed all views from the 5th station at 2'305 meters (7'560 feet). According to my tour guide, this type of weather occurs more than two-thirds of the year (so it is common to have no view, instead of a clear view to the top of the volcano). This makes the mount Fuji touristic daytrip from Tokyo the biggest tourist disappointment, given the fact that the brochures always only show clear and sunny views (the adverse weather conditions are only written in the small print – as if they have a low chance of occurring).

In your travel planning consider that there may be bad weather days and heavy rain, or even typhoons. Typhoon season is May till October with the months of August and September as peak. The rainy season normally starts in June and lasts for about six weeks till end of July. The months after that are very hot with a high humidity, regular rainfall and often clouded skies. During my two-month travel in Japan, in August and September, most of the days were cloudy.

Trash

One of the great experiences are the clean streets, pavements, parks, sightseeing areas, forests, hiking trails, waterways, river streams, and so forth. Even at the top tourist locations where many thousands of foreigners visit, you will find cleanliness.

No rubbish, no dog poop, no spit out gum, no cigarette butts, no plastic bottles, no soft drink cans, no paper, no plastic wrappers, no plastic bags.

Japan's public cleanliness motto is: *Take your trash home.*

As a result, public bins and trashcans are a rarity. You might find them at the main tourist locations, outside the convenience stores, at the main train stations, on the platforms of the main trains stations. However, most public locations do not provide any possibility to dispose of trash. So take your trash back to the hotel, and dispose of it in the bins of your hotel room.

The only exception is the trashcan for the plastic drink bottles or cans from the vending machines. These trashcans have round openings fitting the exact size of the cans and plastic drinks bottles. These bottle bins are always located next to the vending machines. Since there are so many vending machines all over Japan, you will easily be able to get rid of your plastic drink bottles while travelling.

The trash bins on the Shinkansen do not separate trash disposal, but most other, e.g., on the platforms or at the convenience stores, do.

Local Phone/Wi-Fi

Upon your arrival at the international airports in Japan you will see many counters offering local mobile phones and Wi-Fi packages for your stay in Japan. This could indeed be a possibility to reduce your data roaming costs.

Though my personal experience is that you do not need to buy/rent any such sim cards or packages:

- Your accommodations will offer free Wi-Fi. With the free internet calling, e.g., via WhatsApp or Skype, you do not need to incur any telephone costs during the time that you are in your hotel.
- Many cities offer free Wi-Fi around the main tourist locations and the city-center.
- All major department stores offer free Wi-Fi connections.
- Many coffee shops and restaurants offer free Wi-Fi.
- Many apps provide off-line maps, e.g., maps.me or ForeverMap, that you can download prior to your trip. Through the GPS function of your smartphone, these maps can be used to navigate the area where you are travelling or hiking.
- When you rent a car with a navigation system, you should have no troubles with finding your way.

When you are spending most of your day-time sightseeing and travelling, there should really be no need to rent such local mobile phone or Wi-Fi packages for your stay in Japan.

Electrical Plugs

The power sockets in Japan require the same electrical plugs as in the United States: two flat, non-polarised, pins. You will need an adapter in case your appliances have a different electrical plug.

In the newer Shinkansen trains, each seat has its own power outlet to charge your computer, camera, phone or other electronic equipment. The regional and local JR trains, however, do not offer this charging possibility.

Emergency Alerts

Japan has a national emergency warning system that sends warning messages to all mobile phone in the related area for which the warning is made. During my stay in Nagano on 29 August 2017, I received the below warning messages on my smartphone shortly after 6 a.m. Not being able to read Japanese, I had to switch on my computer to find an English language website to check the news. As it turned out, it was a warning for the North Korean missile that flew over Northern Japan at that time.

On 17 September 2017, I received another warning on my smartphone. I was on Shikoku Island, and received a typhoon warning to alert for the approaching Typhoon called "Talim".

Apart from these emergency alerts, I also experienced tremors from an earthquake while in Tokyo at the beginning of August 2017.

Health & Safety

Health and safety is written big in Japan. The speed limits on the roads and expressways are relatively low; the platforms of many busy metro stations and train stations have platform doors to the tracks; people wear facial masks when in public to prevent contaminating other people; at roadworks one or two workers are waving flags to slow down the oncoming traffic; smoking is not allowed in the streets or other public areas; trash must be taken home, and so forth.

Japan is one of the safest countries in the world. If you lose your wallet, phone, camera or luggage, there is a high chance that the finder will drop it off at the lost and found or the nearest location. Theft is very unusual. Of course, you need to look after your belongings just like anywhere else in the world, particularly in the areas with many tourists. But generally speaking, you do not need to take any specific or unusual precautions when visiting Japan.

Some local commuter trains and subway lines may have women-only cars, to protect the women from grappling male commuters during the peak times when the train and subway cars are fully packed.

When you need medication, do bring a sufficient stock with you. Drugstores and pharmacies are relatively rare and difficult to find, and staff may not speak English very well. Even finding regular painkillers may not be easy.

Cash

Bring sufficient foreign currency cash to change into Yen notes, because you will need it. The small villages in the rural areas have no banks where you can change currency, so it is advisable to change upon arrival at the airport.

Some of the bigger towns have banks with international ATMs to withdraw cash, but you would need to coordinate your Yen currency requirements with being at these locations. There are 20'000 7-eleven convenience stores in Japan, in the big and small cities and along the main roads. Each of these 7-eleven stores has a cash withdrawal machine that accepts international credit cards and bankcards. You can withdraw cash from your home country bank account at virtually every street corner. There is no need to enter into the country with large amounts of foreign currency.

Foreign currency exchange counters are available at the main airports and some of the big cities only. The larger hotels usually provide such services as well for the main global currencies. Some of the bigger malls, convenience stores and train stations at tourist locations may have foreign money exchange machines (Automatic Change Machines). You can exchange several foreign currencies (e.g., USD, EUR, CNY), though often only major currencies are accepted. Compared to the ATMs, however, these exchange machines have a very limited presence. Do not count on them too much.

Banks are another possibility of exchanging currency or withdrawing monies. However, generally do not expect that the staff at the counter speaks English, and be aware of the limited opening times and the limited presence in the rural areas.

Accommodations booked directly via English language hotel booking websites likely need to be paid at the time of check-in or check-out. In the more rural areas, it can happen that an accommodation does not accept credit cards, but only cash settlement of the bill.

Many of your drinks can be obtained from the convenience stores or vending machines (often outside the same convenience store or in the hotel lobby). They mostly operate with coins and 1'000 Yen notes.

All bus fares need to be paid in cash.

All metro fares and ropeway fares need to be paid in cash. The metro ticket machines do accept credit cards, but often only local Japanese cards, not the international credit cards.

Some gas stations only accept cash.

Access to most temples, museums and other tourist attractions and sightseeing will have to be paid in cash.

Though the amounts are usually small (apart from the accommodation cash payment), they do add up, especially if you are staying longer than just a few days. In my personal experience, you can easily spend 10'000 Yen (88 USD) in cash daily for food, drinks, admission fees, ropeways, buses, trams, gifts, souvenirs and other small expenditures.

Sales Tax

Depending on your home country, you might be used to seeing the sales prices in stores and restaurants with or without sales tax. In case of the latter, the sales tax is added at the time you pay the bill. In Japan, there is a mix. Many large stores and shops show the prices including the 8 percent sales tax. Still, there are many restaurants and shops that show the sales prices before tax. This can be quite confusing at times.

Language

Apart from a few exceptions, most local people, and particularly the elderly, do not speak any English. That is no problem at all, and makes the communication process adventurous.

At one ryokan, a short old lady served me my breakfast and dinner, and she kept speaking to me in Japanese, even though I could not understand a word. I kept speaking back to her in English with a few Japanese words, but still I think that we understood each other pretty well.

Sometimes, however, you also get lost in translation. On one occasion, the heating was not working in my room, so I called down to the front desk. The first person who answered the phone did not understand my question, so I got connected to three more hotel staff. The fourth staff asked me whether I wanted to know the time of my dinner. I had to go down to the front desk and ask for an English-speaking manager in order to get the problem with the room's heating resolved.

There are many Japanese phrase books that you can buy or useful phrases which you can find on the Internet. The following few phrases and greetings are very helpful in establishing a polite relationship with the local people:

Hello	Konnichi Wa
Good morning	Ohayo Gozaimasu
Good evening	Konban Wa
Thank you	Arrigato Gozaimasu
Thank you very much	Domo Arrigato Gozaimasu
Yes	Hai
Please	Dozo

Excuse me	Sumimasen
I do not understand	Wakarimasen
Goodbye	Sayonara

Friendliness

The Japanese people are extremely friendly and polite to foreigners and to each other. Let me give you some examples from my personal experience.

One late afternoon, after more than 20 kilometers (12.4 miles) hiking, I was very tired, and did not feel like hiking the last three kilometers to my ryokan. I paused at a gas station, and got in discussion with a young man who spoke reasonably well English. I explained my situation, and immediately he made a phone call to my ryokan. I heard him speak in Japanese and heard the word 'gajin', which means foreigner, and he looked at my beard as the hotel manager probably asked for a description of my person. Ten minutes later the hotel manager drove up with the hotel shuttle and brought me back to his ryokan.

At breakfast and dinner, the earlier mentioned short old lady explained all the dishes to me in Japanese, prepared the shabu-shabu and cooked the rice for me on my little table. She put the rice in my bowl, and at some point, even wanted to show me how to eat the rice with the dry seaweed sheets and put the chopsticks in my mouth.

At the front desk of each accommodation they were extremely helpful in sorting out the bus timetables and connections for my travel for the next day. At one ryokan, one of the staff even drove me to the bus stop, and later I saw the manager walk more than a kilometre to the same bus stop with several of his Japanese guests.

During a river boat tour, I met an 83-year-old Japanese man, who had a beautiful walking stick, decorated with mantras in Japanese Kanji characters. Despite his age, the man was very fit. He told me that this was his last pilgrimage and that he had completed his tour of the 88 temples. I had been looking to buy a traditional walking stick for several days, and I was so impressed with his walking stick, that I asked him if I could buy it. He refused, but half an hour later he told me via the tour guide (who translated in English) that he wanted to give me his walking stick for free. I was deeply impressed by the generosity of this kind man, and warmly accepted his kind offer.

One day, late afternoon, I arrived at the tourist office with a need to recharge my phone battery, which was down to 4 percent. I did not have my charger with me, so I asked a staff member of the tourist office if I could use one of theirs. One staff member had a charger in his car, and he offered to take my phone to his car to have it charged there for 30 minutes, which I happily accepted.

ABOUT THE AUTHOR

drs. Hans Beumer is an enthusiastic and seasoned traveller. He has travelled all over the world for business and leisure, exploring many different countries and cultures. Sharing his travel experiences through his travel books enables him to jumpstart the enthusiasm of other people who are looking beyond their local horizons.

Hans travelled to Japan many times, being one of his favourite countries and cultures.

Visit www.hansbeumer.com

Also available from Hans Beumer

In the global traveller series:

In the ultimate happiness series:

www.ingramcontent.com/pod-product-compliance
Lightning Source LLC
LaVergne TN
LVHW091008080826
845145LV00003B/1172

* 9 7 8 3 9 0 6 8 6 1 2 4 1 *